Welcome

We Create our books with love and great care.

Yet mistakes can always happen. For any issues with our book, such as faulty binding, Printing errors, or something else, please do not hesitate to contact us at:
www.facebook.com/kiwianaPublisher

We will make sure you get a replacement copy immediately.

Any suggestions or questions regarding our books, please contact us at
www.facebook.com/kiwianaPublisher

Please support us and leave a review!